J   Heinrichs, Ann
958.1
HEI   Afghanistan

AFGHANISTAN

A TRUE BOOK®

by
Ann Heinrichs

Children's Press®

A Division of Scholastic Inc.

New York Toronto London Auckland Sydney
Mexico City New Delhi Hong Kong
Danbury, Connecticut

An Afghan boy

Content Consultant
David Green
*Journalist and
Nieman Fellow
Harvard University
Boston, MA*

Reading Consultant
Nanci R. Vargus, Ed.D.
*Assistant Professor
Literacy Education
University of Indianapolis
Indianapolis, IN*

*The photograph on the
cover shows a wheat farm
below the Koh-i-Baba
mountain range.
The photograph on the title
page shows a group of
Afghan girls.*

Library of Congress Cataloging-in-Publication Data

Heinrichs, Ann
    Afghanistan / by Ann Heinrichs.
        p. cm. — (A true book)
    Summary: Discusses the geography, history, people, and culture of
Afghanistan.
    Includes bibliographical references and index.
    ISBN 0-516-22775-0 (lib. bdg.)   0-516-27815-0 (pbk.)
    1. Afghanistan—Juvenile literature. [1. Afghanistan.] I. Title. II. Series.
DS351.5 .H45 2003
958.1—dc21   2002008817

Contents

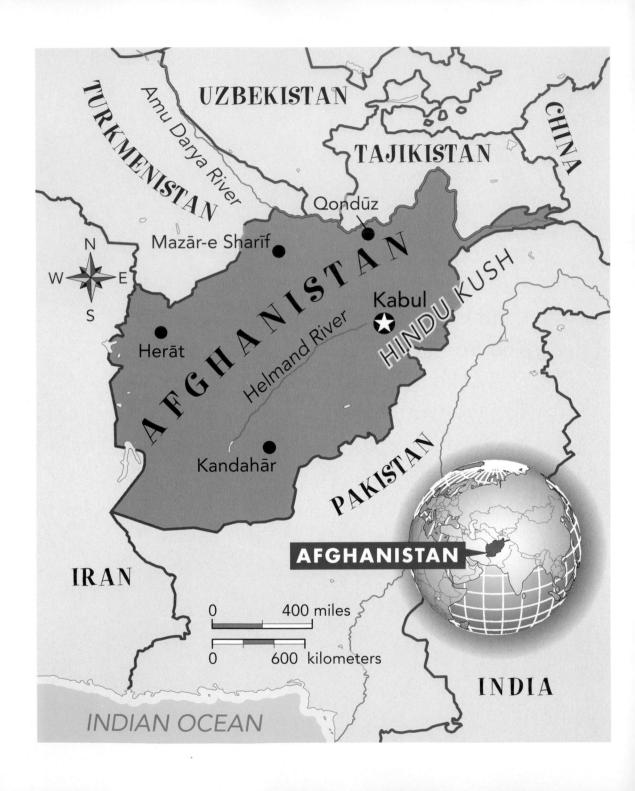

Mountains, Deserts, and Plains

Afghanistan is a land of mountains, deserts, and plains. It is located in south-central Asia. It is shaped like a big leaf with a little stem. Iran lies to the west, and Pakistan is on the east and south. To the north are Turkmenistan, Uzbekistan, and Tajikistan.

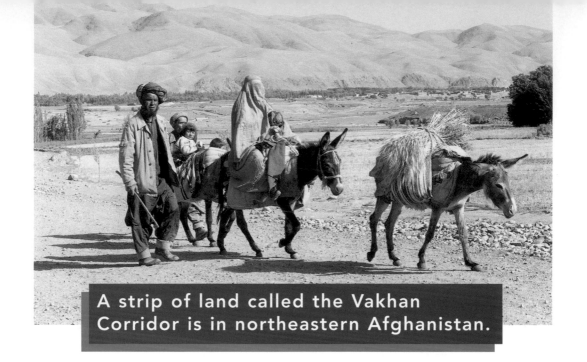

A strip of land called the Vakhan Corridor is in northeastern Afghanistan.

The Vakhan Corridor is the "stem" of the leaf. This narrow strip of land juts out toward the northeast. At the tip of the strip, Afghanistan shares a border with China.

The Hindu Kush Mountains cover much of Afghanistan.

6

Afghanistan is a very mountainous country (left). Snow leopards (above) live in some forests in Afghanistan.

They stretch across the country from northeast to southwest. Their highest peaks are in northeastern Afghanistan. Dense forests cover the high mountainsides. Bears, snow leopards, wolves, and jackals roam through the forests.

Travelers have always had a hard time crossing the Hindu Kush. In a few spots there are passes, or gaps, where people can get through. The Kushan and Khyber passes are well known since ancient times.

High valleys run down the Hindu Kush range. In one valley is Kabul, the capital and largest city. Farther south is Kandahar, the second-largest city.

Rolling hills and fertile plains cover the northwest. Many Afghans live as farmers and

Many people live in Kabul, Afghanistan's capital city.

herders here. The major cities in this region are Mazar-e Sharif and Qonduz. The Amu Darya River forms much of Afghanistan's northern border.

9

Although parts of the country are dry (top), Afghanistan does have some rivers. The Helmand is the largest river in Afghanistan (bottom).

Sandy deserts and high plains cover the south and west. Much of this region is dry, with little

10

vegetation. In the west is Herat, the country's third-largest city. In the south is the Rigestan Desert. The Helmand River is Afghanistan's major river. It flows down from the mountains into southwestern Afghanistan.

Summers are hot and dry, and winters can be bitterly cold. December through March are the wettest months. Then the highlands get snow, while the lowlands get rain. The desert regions, however, get very little rainfall.

Centuries of Change

Through the centuries, many waves of invaders swept through Afghanistan. Aryan people from Central Asia arrived around 1500 B.C. In the 500s B.C., the Persian Empire took over Bactria, now northern Afghanistan. Next came Alexander the Great. His Greek

Alexander the Great was one of the invaders who helped to shape Afghanistan's history.

and Macedonian army invaded in the 300s B.C.

The Kushans of Central Asia arrived around the first century A.D. They introduced the Buddhist religion. Ruins of many Buddhist **monuments** remain from that time. The world's

13

Many of the large Buddha figures in Bamiyan were destroyed.

largest figures of Buddha were carved into a mountainside at Bamiyan. Unfortunately, they were destroyed in 2001 by Afghanistan's Taliban government.

In the 600s, Arab armies introduced their religion of Islam. By about 1000, most people in Afghanistan accepted Islam. It would become the major religion not only in Afghanistan, but in much of this region of the world.

Many other invaders ruled Afghanistan in the years to come. They included the Mongol conqueror Genghis Khan, the Turkic

Genghis Kahn was a famous conqueror who invaded Afghanistan.

Rumi the Poet

Rumi the Poet

Rumi (1207?–1273) was a great poet and spiritual leader. His full name was Jalal ad-Din ar-Rumi. He was born in Balkh, near today's Mazar-e Sharif. Rumi belonged to the mystical Sufi **sect** of Islam and wrote in the Persian language. People all over the world enjoy his poetry. It expresses the soul's love for God.

warrior Timur (Tamerlane), and the Mughal emperors of India. In times of peace, Afghans produced beautiful works of art and poetry.

In 1747, Afghan tribal leaders met in Kandahar. They chose Ahmad Shah Durrani as their king. This was the beginning of a united Afghanistan.

In the 1800s, both Great Britain and Russia hoped to control Afghanistan. Great Britain decided to fight to gain the upper hand. British troops invaded in 1839

British troops invaded Afghanistan during the first Anglo-Afghan War (left). Muhammad Zahir Shah (right) was king during Afghanistan's decade of democracy.

and 1878. These conflicts are called the Anglo-Afghan Wars. At last, in 1919, Afghanistan gained full independence.

In 1963, Afghanistan's "decade of democracy" began.

18

King Muhammad Zahir Shah set out to create a modern state. Women gained many more rights, and many people went to school. However, Zahir's cousin Daoud overthrew him in 1973.

By this time, Russia and several neighboring territories were united as the Soviet Union. Army officers took control of Afghanistan in 1978. They made it a republic with Soviet-style policies. Many Afghans opposed this government. Rebel Afghan groups joined together as the

A group of Afghan warriors receives instructions (above). People celebrate as Soviet tanks leave Afghanistan in the late 1980s (right).

mujahedin, or holy warriors. The Soviets invaded in 1979 to fight them. The United States and several other countries spent millions of dollars to aid the rebels.

After years of warfare, the Soviets left in 1989. Meanwhile,

20

millions of Afghans had fled their homes for safety. Some went to Iran or Pakistan, while others were simply left homeless. To make matters worse, a **drought** had wiped out crops and grazing lands.

The rebels overthrew the government in 1992. Then civil war raged as the rebels fought among themselves. Eventually a group called the Taliban took control. Other Afghan rebel groups formed the Northern Alliance to oppose them. Meanwhile, the Taliban put the country under very strict rule.

The Taliban took control of the Afghan government in the mid-1990s.

They claimed to be religious reformers who were enforcing a pure Islamic way of life. However, the Taliban's rules often had little to do with religion.

The Taliban regime outlawed music, movies, television, kite flying, and even the wearing of squeaky shoes! Men had to wear full beards, and girls could not attend school. Life was especially hard for women in the cities. They were not allowed to hold jobs. In public, they had to wear a dress called the *chadri*. It covered the body completely, from head to toe. Punishments for breaking the rules were brutal.

The Taliban also helped and encouraged a **terrorist** organization called al-Qaeda, led by Osama bin Laden. In 2001, al-Qaeda terrorists destroyed the World Trade Center in New York City. Thousands of people were killed

United States troops (right) joined with the Northern Alliance to overthrow the Taliban government.

in the attack. In response, the United States and other nations joined forces with the Northern Alliance and overthrew the Taliban. International peacekeeping troops arrived to keep order.

Afghanistan needed a stable government. A *loya jirga*, or council of tribal leaders, came together under Hamid Karzai. They agreed to create a new constitution. In 2002, the loya jirga elected Karzai president until democratic elections could be held. One and all, they hoped Afghanistan could begin to heal at last.

Hamid Karzai became the president of Afghanistan in 2002.

Land of Many Cultures

Afghanistan is a land of many **cultures**. About 25 million people live there. They belong to more than twenty **ethnic** groups, each with its own language. Pashto and Dari are the official languages. Both are written in the Arabic script.

The Pashtuns are the largest ethnic group, and they speak

Afghan shepherds with their flock

Pashto. About two out of every five Afghans are Pashtun. They live in the Kandahar region and in the east and south. They live by farming, herding animals, and trading. Pashtuns are organized into tribal groups. Members of each tribe are very loyal to one another.

27

Tajiks are Afghanistan's second-largest ethnic group. About one out of four Afghans is a Tajik. They speak Dari, an Afghan form of the Persian language. Tajik farmers and herders occupy the fertile valleys of the Hindu Kush in the northeast. Others live in western towns or in Kabul.

The Hazara are the third-largest group. They are Mongol people who speak a form of Persian with many Mongol words. They live in the high, rocky regions of central Afghanistan.

A Tajik boy carries corn from his family's farm (above).
A Hazara girl and her sister walk down the street (right).

Several Turkic groups live in Afghanistan, too. Their **ancestors** came from Central Asia. They speak forms of the present-day Turkish language. Uzbeks live as

An Uzbek woman dances during a celebration (above). A group of Turkmen in their native dress gather to talk (right).

farmers and herders on the northern plains. Turkmen live in the far north, along the Amu Darya River. The Kirghiz are **nomads** who live in the Vakhan Corridor.

The Bond of Islam

In spite of ethnic differences, Afghans share religious ties. Almost all Afghans are Muslims, or members of the Islamic faith. They believe in one God, whom they call Allah. Muhammad founded Islam in the 600s. Muslims often call Muhammad the **Prophet**. Muslims also honor

Most Afghans are members of the Islamic faith (above). Three young boys read the Koran together (right).

other prophets known to Christians and Jews. They include Moses, Abraham, and Jesus. The *Qur'an*, or Koran, is Islam's holy book.

For Muslims, religion is a part of everyday life. They pray five times a day, bowing toward Mecca. This city in Saudi Arabia is Islam's holiest site.

Muslims face Mecca when they pray.

Once a year, many Muslims make a *hajj*, or **pilgrimage**, to Mecca. During the month of the hajj is the feast of Eid al-Adha. Muslims all over the world celebrate this feast. It honors Abraham's willingness to sacrifice his son to God. Each family kills a sheep or goat in memory of this sacrifice. Everyone dresses in their finest clothes and enjoys a huge meal.

Another holy time is the month of Ramadan. This is a month of fasting, or going without food,

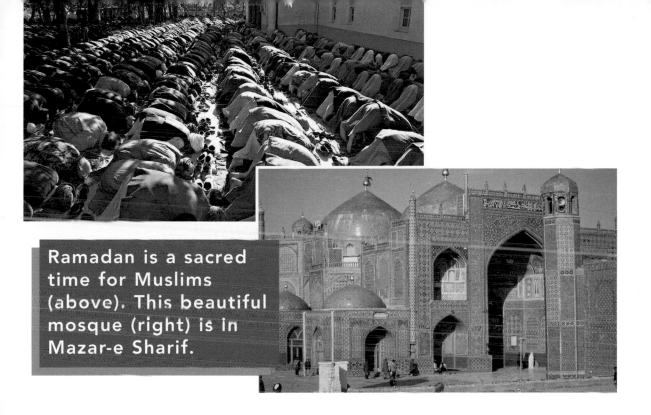

Ramadan is a sacred time for Muslims (above). This beautiful mosque (right) is in Mazar-e Sharif.

from dawn to sunset. At the end of Ramadan comes a three-day celebration called Eid al-Fitr. People gather for prayers, visit relatives, and eat festive meals.

Almost every Afghan village has a **mosque**, or Muslim house of worship. It is filled with worshipers on Friday, the Islamic holy day. Mosques are often beautifully decorated. The mosques at Mazar-e Sharif and Herat are examples. Mullahs are the village priests. They teach Islam to children and apply Islamic law to settle disputes.

Most Afghan Muslims belong to the Sunni branch of Islam. However, the Hazara are a religious **minority**. They are Shi'ite Muslims. Small communities of Hindus, Sikhs, and Christians live in Afghanistan, too.

Daily Life and Traditions

Afghans are friendly and generous people. They serve tea to visitors, even strangers.

Afghans eat round, flat loaves of bread called *naan*. Other foods are yogurt, vegetables, fruit, nuts, and sometimes meat. However, Islamic law forbids alcohol and pork.

An Afghan will often serve his guest tea (above). Houses in rural areas of the country are usually made of mud bricks (right).

About four out of five Afghans live in rural areas, outside of cities. Their homes are built of sun-dried mud bricks. Family ties are strong, and several generations of family members live together. Children help in the fields, tend animals, and take care of younger children.

Nomads live in tents. They move between summer pastures and winter camps. Their animals provide milk, meat, and hides.

Nomads carry all of their belongings from place to place.

Afghan men wear loose-fitting pants and shirts and a turban. Women wear pants, a loose shirt or dress, and a head scarf. Under the Taliban's rule, city women wore the *chadri* in public. In democratic times, women have much more freedom.

Two Afghan girls wear brightly colored clothing.

New Year's Day

Nowruz is New Year's Day in Afghanistan. It falls on the first day of spring. Women prepare two special foods for the festival. One is *samanak*, a sugary dessert. The other is *haft-mehwah*. It is made with seven fruits and nuts as a symbol of springtime.

New Year's is a special time in Afghanistan.

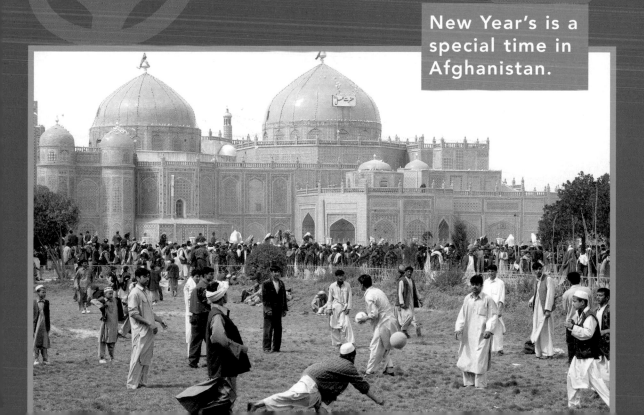

Buzkashi is an ancient sport of northern Afghanistan. Teams on horseback try to get a calf's body past a goal line. Other team sports are soccer and *ghosai*, a type of wrestling. Children play *topay-danda*, a stickball game. They also like flying colorful kites.

Storytelling is an ancient Afghan tradition. Both folktales and tribal histories are passed down from one generation to another. Afghans enjoy traditional folk songs and the *attan*, a rhythmic circle dance. Artisans

Afghan men gather to tell stories (left). Some very fine jewelry is produced in Afghanistan (right).

make beautiful embroidery, jewelry, and carpets.

Afghanistan remains a very poor country. Drought and warfare have left thousands of people hungry, sick, and homeless. Yet, Afghans still express who they are by keeping their **traditions** alive.

To Find Out More

Here are some additional resources to help you learn more about Afganistan:

 **Books**

Ali, Sharifah Enayat. **Afghanistan (Cultures of the World).** Tarrytown, NY: Benchmark Books, 1995.

Chalfonte, Jessica. **I Am Muslim (Religions of the World).** New York: PowerKids Press, 1996.

Juma, Siddiqa. **Stories of the Prophets from the Qur'an.** Elmhurst, NY: Tahrike Tarsile Qur'an, 1998.

Lawrence, McKay and Darryl Ligasan (illus.). **Caravan.** New York: Lee & Low Books, 1995.

Marx, David F. **Ramadan (Rookie Read-About Holidays).** Danbury, CT: Children's Press, 2002.

Mirepoix, Camille (ed.). **Afghanistan in Pictures (Visual Geography).** Minneapolis, MN: Lerner Publications, 1997.

Wood, Angela. **Muslim Mosque (Places of Worship).** Milwaukee, WI: Gareth Stevens, 2000.

Organizations and Online Sites

Center for Afghanistan Studies
University of Nebraska at Omaha
Omaha, NE 68182
1-402-554-2376
http://www.unomaha.edu/~world/cas/cas.html

Afghanistan Online
http://www.afghan-web.com

To learn about the land, people, and culture of Afghanistan.

Afghanistan Culture
http://www.afghan-network.net/Culture/

To learn about Afghanistan's holidays, costumes, ethnic groups, music, and more.

Afghan Info Center
http://www.afghan-info.com

For the latest news, as well as information on women, children, and government leaders.

Important Words

ancestors a person's relatives who lived long ago

culture beliefs, customs, and way of life

drought a long period without rainfall

ethnic relating to a nationality or culture

minority a small number or group within a larger group

monument something built to honor a person or event

nomads people who move their homes from place to place

pilgrimage a journey to a religious place

prophet a person who is believed to speak messages from God

sect one branch of beliefs within a religion

terrorists people who use violence to get their way

traditions the customs and beliefs of a group of people

Index

Meet the Author

Ann Heinrichs grew up in Arkansas and lives in Chicago, Illinois. She has written more than eighty books about American, European, Asian, and African history and culture. Several of her books have won national and regional awards.

Besides the United States, she has traveled in Europe, North Africa, the Middle East, and east Asia. The desert is her favorite terrain.

Ms. Heinrichs holds bachelor's and master's degrees in piano performance. She practices t'ai chi empty-hand and sword forms and has won many awards in martial arts competitions.